The Story of Hubbard's Hills

by

David N Robinson OBE

Published to mark the Centenary of the gift of Hubbard's Hills to the people of Louth on 1st August 1907

Published by

Louth Naturalists', Antiquarian and Literary Society

Louth Museum, 4 Broadbank, Louth, Lincs LN11 0EQ
tel: 01507 601211 email: louthmuseum@btconnect.com
2007

ISBN 978-0-9539533-4-9

Hubbard's Hills from the air, 2001
(inside front cover)

and Hubbard's Hills, 2002
(back cover)

Courtesy East Lindsey District Council

Printed by Cupit Print, The Ropewalk, 23 Louth Road, Horncastle, Lincolnshire LN9 5ED

Cattle grazing by the stream in the valley bottom, 1905.
(Published by Jay Em Jay of Grimsby. Printed in Belgium)

A Jay Em Jay multiview postcard published shortly after formal establishment of the park in 1907.
Sold by William Lacey & Co. Stationers, 74/76 Eastgate, Louth

Than Hubbard's Hills a fairer spot can scarce be found in Lincoln's shire

C. Donner, 1896

THE picturesque valley known perversely as Hubbard's Hills is on the west side of Louth and just within the Lincolnshire Wolds Area of Outstanding Natural Beauty. The valley is a classic open-ended glacial meltwater channel, the most spectacular of dozens of similar features in the chalk landscape of the eastern Wolds. For this reason it is designated as a Regionally Important Geomorphological Site.

Towards the end of the Ice Age, in what is known as the Devensian period, about 20,000 years ago, glaciers from Northern England, Scotland and Scandinavia again invaded east Lincolnshire. Some 100,000 years previously the edge of the Wolds had been a sea cliff of chalk (similar to those on the south coast of Kent and Sussex today), and was still steep, but the ice managed to penetrate the Hallington and Welton valleys. The ice was some 150 feet at its thickest, about the height of the gallery at the base of the spire of St James's church in Louth.

As the climate began to warm up again, the decaying ice (down to about 50 feet thick) and its deposits of boulder clay (till) in the Hallington valley impeded the immense quantities of spring-time snow-melt waters pouring off the Wolds and ponded them back into an extensive lake. The lake water overflowed northwards across the chalk ridge descending as a waterfall into the Welton valley. The waterfall quickly worked its way southwards to create the Hubbard's Hills gorge. Such was the force and erosive capability of the water that it took little more than 250-300 years to slice right through the ridge of well jointed and frost-shattered chalk and drain the Hallington lake.

At the north end of the gorge a decaying block of ice in the Welton valley diverted the water east, which then escaped south, at first beneath the main decaying ice sheet and then between the receding ice front and the steep edge of the Wolds. The boulder clay deposits in the lower Hallington valley ensured the permanent diversion of the Hallington Beck (fed also by the Raithby/Tathwell Beck and its tributaries), meandering on the former lake bed before tumbling over a stony bed of rapids into the gorge where it developed a natural winding course as weathering also reduced the original near-vertical sides. There were small waterfalls along the beck in the valley, the beck was also braided into two courses in places and additionally was fed by springs in the valley floor.

The steepest valley-side slopes today are on the outside of the two main bends, with shallower slopes of original bed load deposits on the inside of the bends. At the north end of the gorge the chalk cliff is probably the result of construction of the present roadway in the 1870s. The exposure shows a pink band in the Lower

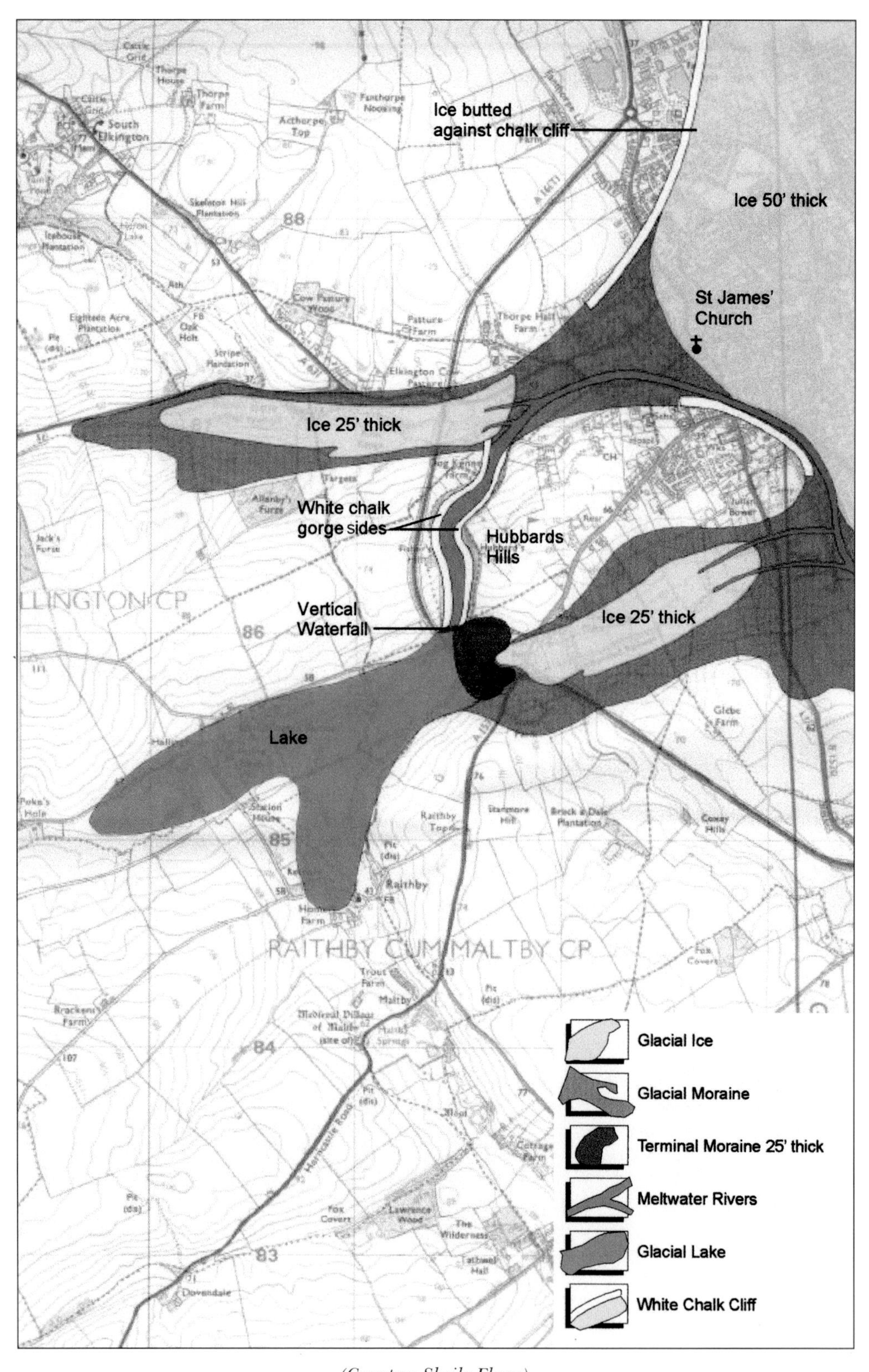

(Courtesy Sheils Flynn)

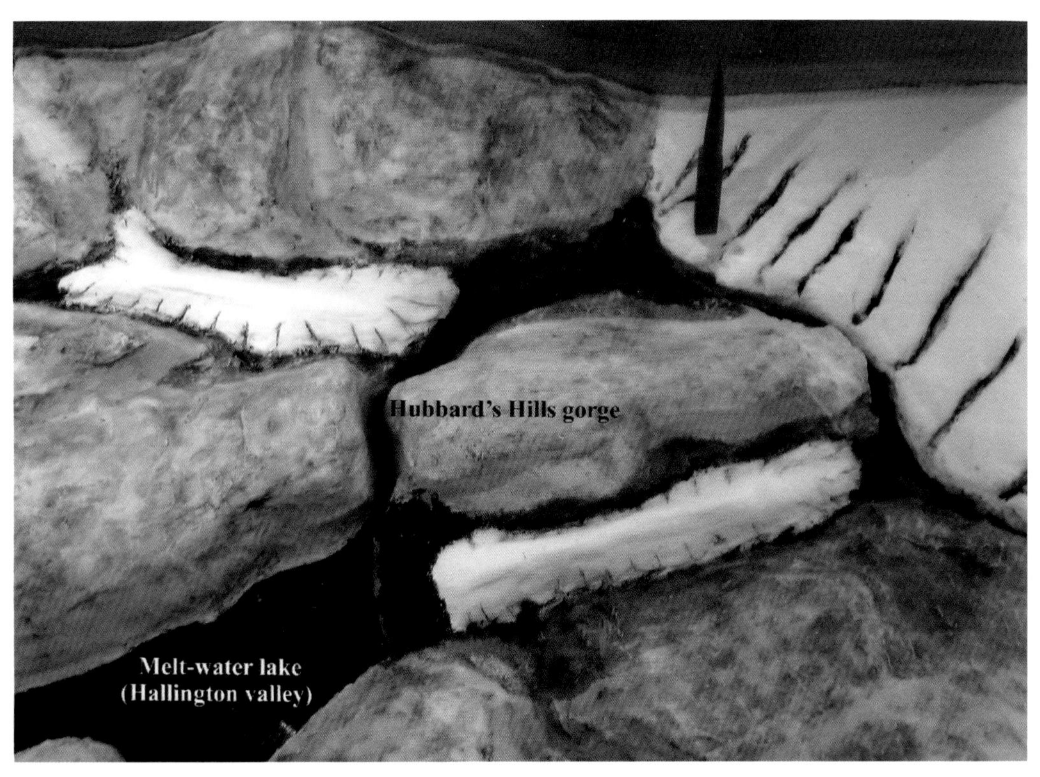

The making of Hubbard's Hills gorge

The model above in Louth Museum and the map opposite show how the snow melt-water trapped by the decaying ice overflowed the chalk ridge to cut the gorge. The simple representation of the tower and spire of St James's church gives an indication of the thickness of the main mass of ice.

At an earlier period of the Ice Age mammoths roamed the Wolds. Mammoth teeth are on display in Louth Museum.

Chalk, the underlying Red Chalk and Carstone being the bedrock (covered by boulder clay and alluvium) of the Hallington valley. As the slopes reduced in steepness in post-glacial times they were colonised by chalk downland grasses and scrub.

Stone Age, Bronze Age and Iron Age peoples had little use for the valley except for hunting and as a water supply downstream, and the Romans ignored it. Saxon and Danish settlement of the area resulted in the establishment of parish boundaries, that between Louth and Hallington running along the top of the east (Hubbard's Hill) side of the valley. On the Louth side the Hallington and Welton Becks join to form the River Lud, flowing along the north side of the valley and forming the parish boundary with South Elkington. The gentler slope on the south side – now Westgate Fields – was grazed, while to the south again were the medieval strip ploughlands of the open South Field. There was a narrow extension of Louth parish down the slope of Hubbard's Hill to the Hallington Beck, probably to give access to a medieval water mill.

At the time of the Domesday Survey in 1086, no woodland was recorded for Hallington parish. The floor of the valley provided cattle grazing, but the sides were too steep for sheep and scrubbed up with gorse. There was probably little change through medieval, Tudor and Stuart times. Even towards the end of the eighteenth century Armstrong's map of 1776-78 shows no woodland, although elsewhere woodlands are clearly marked; similarly there were no trees on the valley slopes on John Cary's map of Lincolnshire in 1801. Arthur Young's report to the Board of Agriculture in 1799 described other parts of the chalk Wolds as areas of sheep walks and rabbit warrens. The Louth-Horncastle turnpike through Louth's South Field had opened in 1770. The Stanmore tollhouse was moved to its present position in 1781 to prevent illegal use of the road to Hallington which changed its name from Tinker Lane to Halfpenny Lane.

By the second half of the eighteenth century the ownership of all Hallington parish (1,948 acres) was in the hands of the Chaplins of Tathwell and Blankney, who were also lords of the manor. The land in Hallington along with most of the adjoining parishes of Raithby and Tathwell had been owned by the Hambys of Tathwell until John Chaplin married Elizabeth Hamby in 1658. Thomas Chaplin bought Blankney in 1719 which became the principal family seat.

As Hallington parish was in single ownership enclosure was done privately, presumably by the Chaplins in the late eighteenth century, with coverts and copses to provide good foxhunting country. By the 1840s there were two main tenant farmers – George Allenby and Richard Chatterton. Thomas Cole was at Dog Kennel Farm with meadow pasture in the valley bottom, and Edward Hackforth, the corn miller at the watermill, also rented similar pasture, and both had a 'cabbage garden' in the valley. Charles Chaplin treated his lands in east Lincolnshire as a sporting estate for hunting, shooting and other country pursuits, particularly hare coursing at Tathwell from 1806, for which he bred greyhounds.

By 1805 the Louth open fields and common pasture had been enclosed under an Act of Parliament (1801). The Award map shows what is now Westgate Fields as four old enclosures (one was called World's End Close), with a shelterbelt of trees planted to separate them from the old South Field. Crowtree Lane was laid out along this boundary, probably the line of an existing track. This gave access to new enclosures, particularly one of nearly four acres, abutting Westgate Fields and Hallington parish, allotted to Charles Chaplin.

The enclosure Commissioners decreed that a 15-feet wide private carriage road be laid out diagonally across Chaplin's allotment to Whitworth Hill Road of similar width – a length of 105 yards 'into Hallington parish'. The Award map shows no detail of Hallington parish except the line of the river and the watermill, but the Whitworth Hill 'Road' would have connected with a diagonal path down the valley slope known later as the Devil's Walk. However, the private carriage road over the brow of the hill was not really practical and instead Crowtree Lane was extended down to the watermill. Perhaps Chaplin had a say in this as it was his mill. The headrace had been created by building a brick sluice in the river to give a head of water which could be released when required to drive the breast-shot waterwheel. The tailrace then directed the water back into the winding river. The tenant from the 1820s to 1840s was Edward Hackforth, who had a shop and bakehouse in Eastgate, Louth and also rented the Chaplin allotment on the other side of the road.

It seems likely that the Devil's Walk was part of a cross-country footpath from Louth through Hubbard's Hills to Hallington. However, in 1826 the Corporation voted £5 towards the expense of 'forming a foot road round Hubbard's Hills and across the Hallington Road'; that is the present path along the top of the east side of the valley and incorporating the former Whitworth Hill 'Road' where the path is now noticeably wider. By this time the name Hubbard's Hills seems to have been firmly established, the hill on the east side having been named after tenant farmer Alexander Hubbard who died in Hallington in 1793. The hill on the west side is Fisher's Hill, presumably named after another tenant.

Dog Kennel Farm was built shortly after 1826. The South Wold Hunt had been formed in 1822 out of the Brocklesby which had formerly hunted the whole of the Wolds, and this was one of four kennels used by the new Hunt (the others being at Horncastle, Hundleby and Harrington) until the new Belchford Kennels were built in 1857. It is not surprising to find a kennels built on Chaplin land conveniently close to Louth, as Charles was a keen supporter of fox hunting. A steeplechase course was nearby in the Hallington valley with seven fences and the beck – named variously Hallington or Whitworth – to be cleared seven times. (Perhaps Whitworth was the name of another sometime tenant farmer.) The kennels farm was accessed by a track from the Elkington road and through the Thorpe Hall estate via the stableyard to the west of the Hall; the bridle road continued through Hubbard's Hills on the west side of the river to Halfpenny Lane.

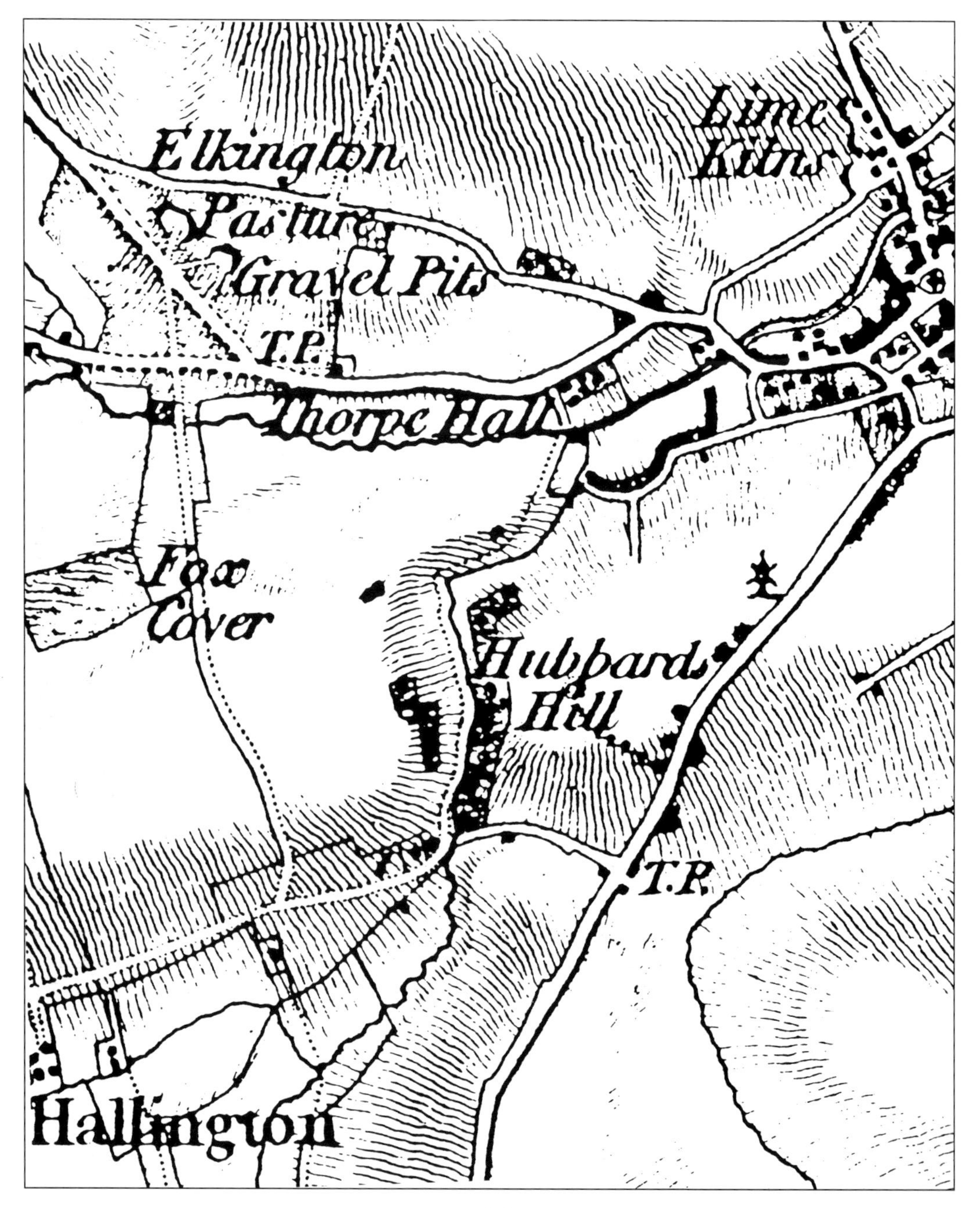
Elkington
Pasture
Gravel Pits
Lime
Kilns
T.P.
Thorpe Hall
Fox
Cover
Hubbard
Hill
T.P.
Hallington

1824

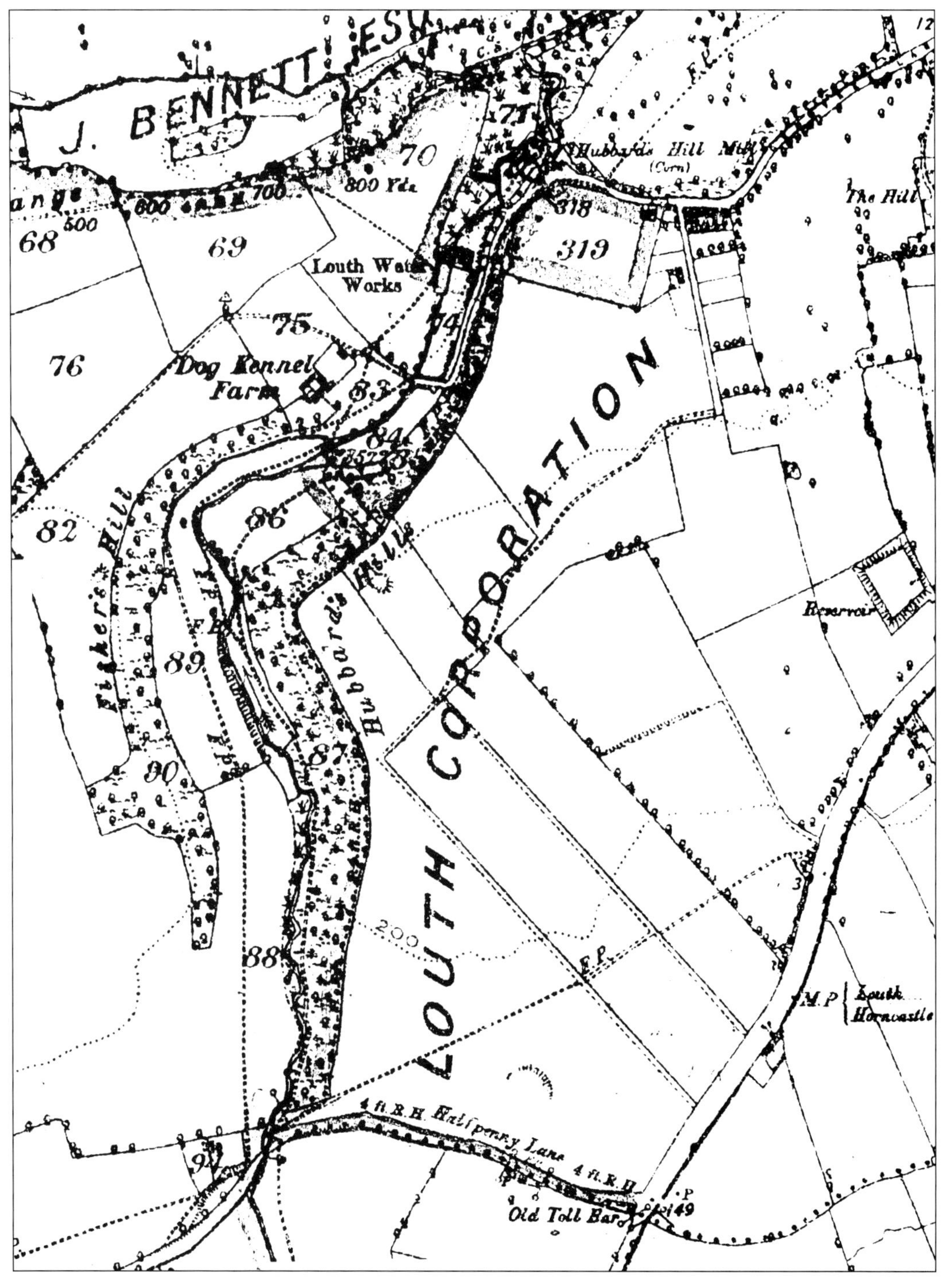
J. BENNETT ESQ
Hubbard's Hill Mill
(Corn)
The Hill
800 Yds
700
600
500
68
69
70
71
318
319
Louth Water Works
75
74
76
Dog Kennel Farm
83
84
82
86
Fisher's Hill
Hubbard's Hill
LOUTH CORPORATION
Reservoir
89
90
87
88
200
F.P.
M.P
Louth
Horncastle
4 ft. R.H. Halfpenny Lane 4 ft. R.H.
Old Toll Bar
149
92

1905

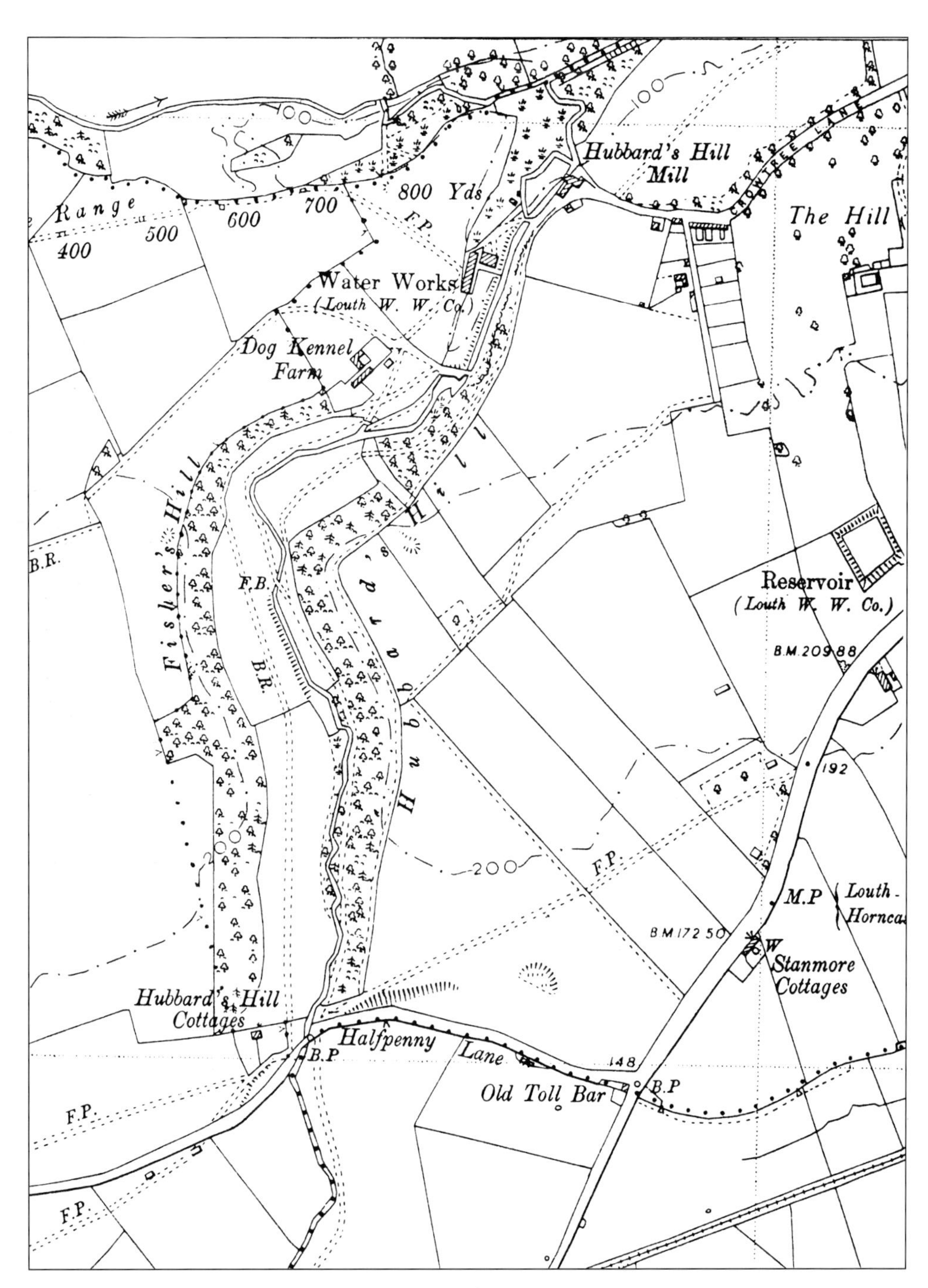
Range
400
500
600
700
800 Yds
F.P.
Hubbard's Hill Mill
The Hill
Water Works
(Louth W. W. Co.)
Dog Kennel Farm
Fisher's Hill
Hubbard's Hill
F.B.
B.R.
B.R.
Reservoir
(Louth W. W. Co.)
B.M. 209.88
192
F.P.
200
M.P
Louth
B.M. 172.50
W
Stanmore Cottages
Hubbard's Hill Cottages
Halfpenny Lane
B.P
148
Old Toll Bar
B.P
F.P.
F.P.

1947

View north-east from Fisher's Hill. Dog Kennel Farm in foreground and Chaplin's Mill to the left. Windmill was on Little Crowtree Lane. Note conifer plantings in foreground and on east (Hubbard's Hill) side of the valley.
J. W. Wilson, 1840

Along the bridle road through the Valley, with Dog Kennel Farm upper left and conifers on the slope of Hubbard's Hill.
J. W. Wilson, 1840

The southern entrance to the Valley from Halfpenny Lane.
J. W. Wilson, 1840 *(see page 17)*

Westgate Fields.
J. W. Wilson, 1840

EVIDENCE of the appearance and management of Hubbard's Hills and Westgate Fields in the mid-nineteenth century comes from the engraved drawings by Louth solicitor James William Wilson (published in 1840), the Louth Panorama sketched and painted by William Brown (1844-47) and the Hallington Tithe Award and map (1852), together with the 1st edition One Inch Ordnance Survey 1824 (surveyed 1820) and C & J Greenwood's county map on a similar scale (1827-28). These show that there were hedges dividing the cattle pasture fields in the valley bottom, with mature trees in the hedges and by the river banks. The valley sides were being planted up by the 1820s, and the 1840 engravings show conifers, quite densely planted particularly on the steepest eastern slope at the south end. The conifer plantings are also clearly depicted in regular rows on Brown's Panorama.

The reason for planting conifers was probably economic. It was being done on other Lincolnshire estates, notably at Brocklesby, and would have been suitable for shallow soils and steep slopes. Arthur Young's report in 1799 had noted that Scots pine, spruce and larch planted as two-year old seedlings at 1,200 to the acre could produce a return in fifteen years with timber for farmhouses and barns and thinnings for fence rails and firewood. At Hubbard's Hills the plantings were 'in hand', that is not let to tenants, which implies that Charles Chaplin himself was the instigator of the plantings. Perhaps he also considered that they had value as cover for game.

Wilson's engravings were numbered and published in a set of twelve as Sketches of Louth. They were in the tradition of picturesque views fashionable from the late eighteenth to the mid-nineteenth century. It is significant that of the twelve, three were of Hubbard's Hills and one of Westgate Fields, indicating that the area was already regarded as a beauty spot and had become a popular destination for visitors. The engraving of the southern entrance to the valley shows the beck as a ford across Halfpenny Lane, a wooden footbridge, the start of the bridle road through the valley on the west side, and on the east slope well-worn foot tracks down from the valley-top 'foot road' (with figures perambulating on it). A photograph of the same view about 1900 shows a brick bridge in place of the ford, and a wide eroded chalky track down the east slope that had needed to be reinforced with wooden steps at the top because of regular use.

Another of Wilson's sketches was of Westgate Fields sloping down to the River Lud, looking towards the town and showing dividing hedges, clumps of trees, sheep grazing and an angler on the river bank. Brown's Panorama shows a clearly defined footpath through the Fields, with figures walking on it, from Westgate to Chaplin's watermill, sheep and horses grazing and a cottage in the field next to the mill. Wilson's view also shows a row of ten tall posts, used by the town washerwomen as a drying ground. As for the River Lud, it was, according to the writer of *Notices of Louth* (R S Bayley, 1834), 'remarkable for nothing except trout, watercress and rats'. The fact that the boundary between the north and south electoral wards of Louth, established after the 1835 Municipal Corporation Act, followed the path through Westgate Fields confirms that it was a well-established pedestrian link between the town and Hubbard's Hills.

Charles Chaplin visited Tathwell and his estate at Hallington in the 1850s, perhaps to view his plantations at Hubbard's Hills. He was quite an autocrat and a terror to poachers. However he had no children, and after his death all the estates (25,000 acres including Blankney, Metheringham, Temple Bruer and Scopwick in the west of the county) were inherited by his nephew Henry Chaplin on his 21st birthday in 1862. Henry was to become a Member of Parliament, Privy Counsellor and Deputy Lieutenant for Lincolnshire. Like his uncle he enjoyed hunting, racing horses, country sports and entertaining lavishly. Within thirty years his finances were severely embarrassed, and the problem of cutting expenses to match diminishing resources was beyond him. It would eventually affect the ownership of the Hallington lands.

The Louth Waterworks Company, formed in 1871, bought one acre of valley bottom land from Chaplin and bored down 58 feet at the location of the Silver Springs, through silt, sand and clay, White Chalk and Red Chalk into the Carstone. Water was found at a depth of 17 to 25 feet. The works were designed by the well-known Louth architect James Fowler and built in 1872-73 (twice the size of the surviving building) with steam to pump the water up to a reservoir on the crest of the Horncastle Road to supply the town by gravity.

This however was not good news for the tenant of the watermill, William Hall and his son Bryan. They could no longer build up a head of water in the river, and water abstraction would also have diminished the supplementary flow of the Silver Springs. Therefore they constructed the reservoir in 1877 by building a dam, and straightened the river course below to the mill headrace. It seems likely that the roadway alongside the new course was made at the same time to give access to Dog Kennel Farm across the bridge dam.

The passing of the Bank Holiday Act in 1871 and the opening of the Louth to Bardney railway through the Wolds in 1876, with connections to Lincoln, resulted in Louth and Hubbard's Hills becoming a popular destination for excursions during the city's Foundry Trip Week which led up to the August Bank Holiday (then the first Monday in the month). The normal journey from Lincoln, four passenger trains a day each way stopping at all intermediate stations, took just over an hour. To save a few pence passengers might get off at the small Hallington station to walk to Hubbard's Hills, a shorter distance than from Louth station. Local folk went through Westgate Fields to Hubbard's Hills for a Sunday stroll or a summer picnic.

The 'Hills' were also being explored by naturalists, particularly the Louth Naturalists' Club, founded by five teenagers in 1884 and now the Louth Naturalists', Antiquarian and Literary Society. The Society's first museum curator, Charles Smith Carter, investigated the chalk exposures in 1899 and for a number of years studied molluscs in the river, both before and after the making of artificial cascades in 1907 (see page 41) which affected the distribution of species, and in the soil wash at the foot of Fisher's Hill. His studies of molluscs in Hubbard's Hills formed the basis of his second Presidential Address to the Lincolnshire Naturalists' Union in 1929.

continued on page 23

The view from the top of the steps and chalky track down the east side of the valley to Halfpenny Lane, with more tracks on the far side of the beck. A Valentine Series card, 1903, sold by A. Cappin, Eastgate, Louth

A photograph about 1900 of the bridge over the Hallington Beck, with the well-worn chalky track down the valley side showing the extent of its use.

Down by the riverside
1906

The Hallington Beck cascades into the valley at the south end.
Published by Charles Parker, Stationer, Market Place, Louth, 1905.

There were at least eight versions of this popular viewcard, photographed with two little girls at the foot of the tree in 1903, and still selling in 1916. W. Lacey & Co and A. Coppin of Louth both sold them.

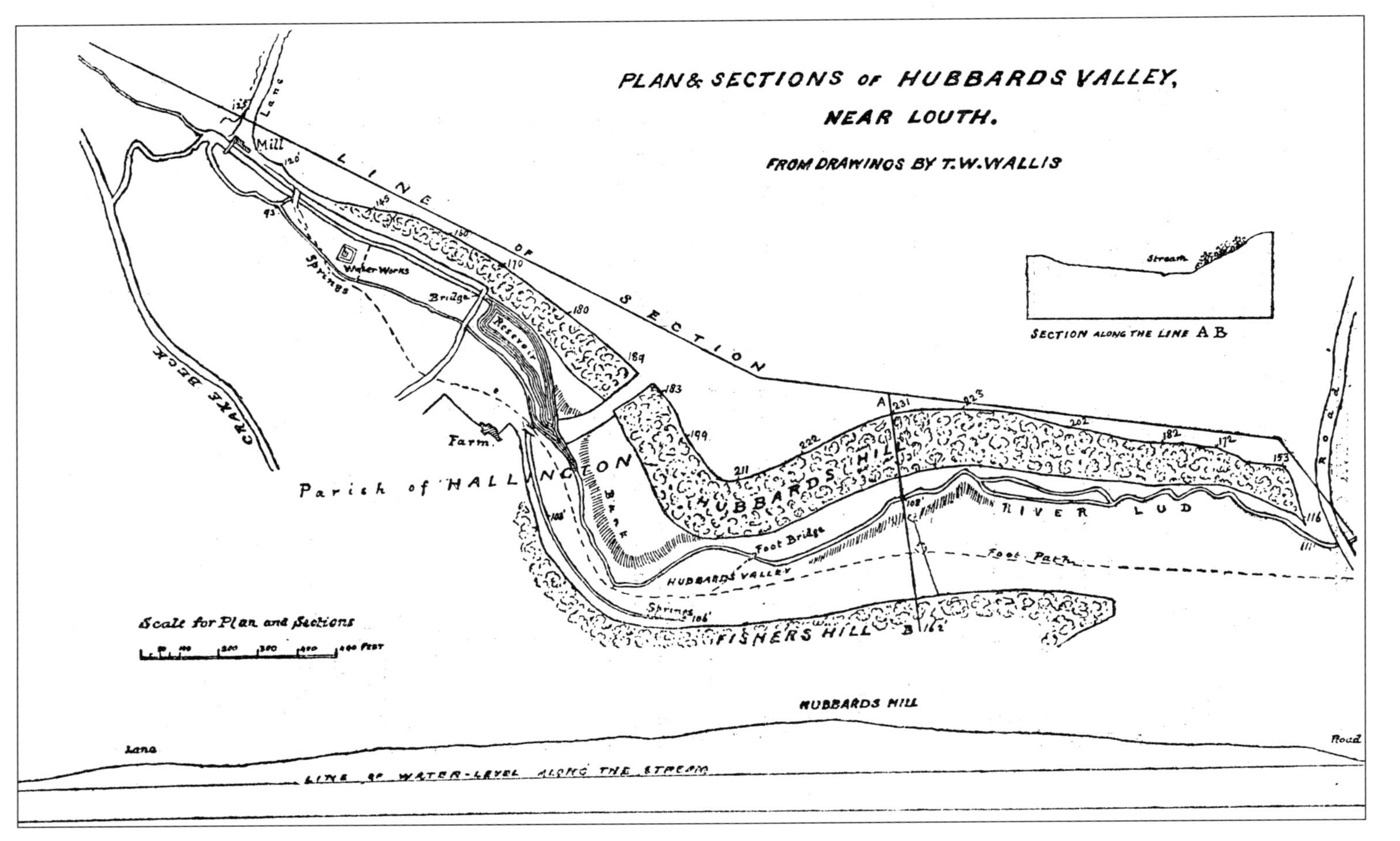
PLAN & SECTIONS OF HUBBARDS VALLEY,
NEAR LOUTH.
FROM DRAWINGS BY T.W. WALLIS
Lane
Mill
LINE OF SECTION
Water Works
Springs
Bridge
Reservoir
Stream
SECTION ALONG THE LINE AB
Road
CRAKE BECK
Farm
Parish of HALL NGTON
Bank
HUBBARDS HILL
RIVER LUD
Foot Bridge
Foot Path
HUBBARDS VALLEY
Springs
FISHERS HILL
Scale for Plan and Sections
HUBBARDS HILL
Lane
Road
LINE OF WATER-LEVEL ALONG THE STREAM

1887

In 1884 William Mawer of Louth published a little booklet *How the River Lud Cut Through Hubbard's Hills*, with a title page engraving of a genteel couple by the lake (see page 65), as a tribute to his late schoolmaster George Tagg who had taken him and others on rambles there. It was addressed to 'the townspeople of Louth who are so justly proud of their walks – the young and old who direct their rambles through these favourite spots', and he referred to Hubbard's Hills and Welton Vale as ravines, 'altogether exceptional phenomena in chalk districts'. Three years later, in 1887, a Geological Survey Memoir *The Geology of part of East Lincolnshire* by A J Jukes-Browne was published in which he included a chapter on the hills and valleys of the Wolds and a plan and section of Hubbard's Valley based on drawings by Louth's renowned woodcarver and Borough Surveyor Thomas Wilkinson Wallis. The cross-section demonstrates the asymmetry of the valley, and the plan shows the braided nature of the river, location of springs and additional flow along the foot of the steep slope of Fisher's Hill. It also marks the footpath through the valley west of the river and a footbridge over it, but no path on the east side of the river.

By 1897 Henry Chaplin was no longer able to meet the mortgage payments on his estates at Blankney, Tathwell and Hallington, found himself in negative equity and was obliged to transfer them to the Earl of Londesborough. Most of the Hallington lands were then sold at auction in 1905 to William Chatterton, a former tenant who also farmed at Welton le Wold, and to John William Ward of Withcall including the watermill (then tenanted to John Teasdale who had installed a supplementary steam engine in the mid-1880s), the mill dam and $17^1/2$ acres of grazing land in the Hubbard's Hills valley. (Ward also acquired the former Chaplin estate in Raithby parish.)

A couple (lower right) walk on the path through Westgate Fields, where horses gambol and sheep graze, towards Chaplin's Mill, and beyond are serried ranks of conifers on Hubbard's Hill, as painted by William Brown on the Louth Panorama, 1847

The coloured version of the picture on the 1903 postcard described opposite.
This card was posted in Louth in January 1905 to Grimsby; the first part of the message reads:
'Thought I must just send to see if you are alive yet'.

On early postcards, this one postmarked August 1904, only the address could be
written on the back – hence the birthday message on the front.
Printed in Saxony and sold by Charles Parker, Market Place, Louth.

THE popularity of the Hills and its network of footpaths before 1907 is demonstrated by the number of different published picture postcard views. It is also an indication of the willingness of the new owners to allow access to their land on what had become public footpaths. At least thirty picture postcards were on sale prior to the Hills becoming an offical public park. One shows the reservoir, two children fishing with stick and string, the farm gate and Dog Kennel Farm. The message on the back reads: 'Miss E Casson and I cycle to Louth 12 Sept 1903. After dinner we call on Mr [Charles] Luck who accompanies us over the fields [Westgate] to Hubbard's Hills. We return through the valley portrayed on this p.c. and have tea with Mr L at the Royal Oak [on Upgate].' A different card of the same year carried the message 'Hubbard's Hills is a lovely place & within a quarter of an hour's walk from our house.'

Other views are of the Kennels Farm Road, Hallington (Halfpenny) Lane at the south end, trodden paths along the east bank with a simple seat, cattle grazing, and the river showing rapids and a small waterfall. The most popular view was of the simple wooden footbridge over the river, of which there were at least ten different versions, with or without people in the picture. Valentine was the main publisher, but others were sold by local stationer and bookseller Charles Parker of Market Place, Louth (printed in Saxony and Belgium). Taken with the post-1907 viewcards, they provide an historical record of landscape changes.

The message on the September 1903 postcard indicates what was most likely the regular informal circuit of the Hills before as well as after 1907. From opposite the watermill the path ascended Hubbard's Hill, with the precipitous valley side on the right and glimpses through the trees of the reservoir and meadows in the valley bottom. The path broadens to a dramatic viewpoint where it bends left and follows the top of the slope to the limit of the wooded valley side before descending to Halfpenny Lane. Return was along the east side of the river, crossing it by the footbridge and carrying on past the farm and reservoir and along the farm access road back to the starting point.

The 2nd edition of the 25 inch Ordnance Survey published in 1906 shows the top path, the footpath on the east side of the river, paths on both sides of the river north of the footbridge, and the bridle road from Halfpenny Lane to Dog Kennel Farm. The reservoir is shown as silted up at the southern end where the river slows down and drops its load. The woods on the slopes of Fisher's Hill were predominantly broadleaved, while on the east side deciduous trees mingled with conifers, particularly towards the southern end. This would imply that much of the conifer plantations had been felled.

A Sunday stroll to Hubbard's Hills along the Chalk Road beside the mill dam section of the river.
On the left is the Waterworks building.
Photographed and printed by the Cotswold Publishing Co, Wootton under Edge, Glos.

Where the river enters the reservoir. Dog Kennel Farm is on the left.
The chimney on the skyline centre left is for the pumping engine at the Waterworks.
Photograph by Harrison of Lincoln, 1904.

Posed at the northern end of the Top Walk.
Published by W.H. Smith, 1909.

Near the southern end of the Low Walk, about 1906.
The boy seated on the right also appears on the bridge on page 35.

Devil's Walk crosses the slope at an angle, 1906

Top Walk, 1908

Two sepia studies of the Valley and the Low Walk in the 1920s.

Published by J. Nock, Stella Road, London.

Artificial waterfall towards the south end.

1908

Riffles in the river towards the south end.

Published by Clark & Son, Louth

The Low Walk near the Halfpenny Lane entrance about 1926.
Note the fallen tree across the river left.
Published by William Clarke, Mablethorpe.

A pleasant place to sit in the summer shade by the beck as it
tumbled over one of the small artificial waterfalls in the mid-1930s.
This card was posted on 22 May 1938 by Ivy and Fred on a hiking holiday.

Canon A. S. Wilde

Ald. F. J. Ingoldby

Auguste Alphonse Pahud

Mayor of Louth Cllr Richard Dawson

Ald. Henry Simpson

THIRTY years earlier, in 1875, an immigrant from Switzerland arrived in Louth whose fate would determine the future of Hubbard's Hills. He was Auguste Alphonse Pahud (pronounced Pihud) MA, who came to teach French and German at the King Edward VI Boys' Grammar School. He was on the staff only a short time, during which he became attached to Annie Grant, only daughter of William and Maria Grant, a wealthy farming family with homes at The Limes, Westgate and The Manor, Withern. Following teaching appointments in Middlesborough, Cardiff and King's College, London, Auguste and Annie married in 1887 (he was 39 and she was 45) and they lived at The Limes. He gave up teaching and they spent several months a year travelling. He was made a county magistrate in 1894, but took little part in local affairs. They were inseparable and when Annie died suddenly in London in 1899, when they were on the way to the continent to improve her health, Auguste's life was broken, he became severely depressed and was treated for insomnia and melancholia and rarely went beyond his garden at The Limes. On 31 July 1902 he made his will and on 5 August committed suicide by hanging himself with the cord of his dressing gown. He was 53.

The gross value of his estate was £24,751. After bequests to relatives and others, the rest of the estate after expenses was to be paid over to seven trustees to distribute the proceeds 'between the charitable and religious objects of the Parish of Louth and the Parish of Withern as they think will be best and will be most appropriate to perpetuate the memory of my late dear wife, provided always that the amount of money devoted to non-religious charitable objects shall not be less than two-thirds of the whole surplus monies held by the trustees'. The trustees were Rev Arthur Smythe, Vicar of Sutton on Sea (then owner of Brown's Panorama of Louth) and Frederick John Ingoldby, solicitor (of Bell, Ingoldby, Wilson & Son) and Borough Councillor – the executors, and the following office holders at the time of Pahud's death: Mark Smith, Mayor of Louth, Canon Albert Sydney Wilde, Rector of Louth, Rev Frederick Augustus Glover, Rector of Withern, Rev Frederick Freshney (of Withcall), Chairman of the Guardians of the Poor of the Louth Union and William Walliss Wells, Chairman of the Guardians of the Poor in the Parish of Withern. It is to those gentlemen that is owed the idea and acquisition of Hubbard's Hills for the town, but the object took some time to achieve and was not without its difficulties.

£1,000 was assigned for the creation of a memorial window to Mrs Pahud in the clerestory of the north side of the chancel of St James's church, three almshouses were built in Withern for parishioners over 60 years of age (with each receiving five shillings a week), The Limes became the base for the Girls' Grammar School, which moved there in September 1904, and scholarships were created, and grants amounting to about £1,700 were made to the School and to Louth Hospital (on Crowtree Lane). A High Court ruling had to be obtained in 1906 to ensure that the devotion of part of the Trust Fund for providing a public park for Louth was within the terms of the will.

Obtaining a judgement in their favour, the trustees purchased 35 acres 3 roods 28 perches from J W Ward, lord of the manor of Hallington, for £2,025 (just over £56 an acre), including the reservoir and the watermill and garden. (Dog Kennel

continued on page 41

A picnic on the simple wooden footbridge about 1900.
Note the worn paths on the slope beyond.

The Bridge

A Valentine view of 1902 shows part of the central support of the bridge broken. Two boys sit on the bank (right) while two girls prepare to paddle in the stream – and a companion card shows them doing so.

The Bridge

A rare view (above) of the replacement flat structure just before the bow bridge with rustic rails was built in 1907. Note the grazing sheep.

The Bridge

Two charming posed pictures just before the Great War – in winter with leafless trees silhouetted on Fisher's Hill, and in summer with five well-dressed girls.

A flat bridge with simple rustic rails and a handgate replaced the bow bridge swept away in the 1920 flood.

The Bridge

An alternative way of crossing the river: Nottingham University geography students in summer 1952.

The Pahud Memorial Fountain as it looked shortly after construction in 1907, and before completion of fences and gates.
Published by J.W. Goulding & Son, Stationer, 20 Mercer Row, Louth.

An unusual view of the Memorial Fountain from the slope of Fisher's Hill, about 1909.

The Memorial Fountain and bridges, with sheep still grazing, about 1909.

By the mid-1930s the ornamental planting in front of the Fountain had grown up, and the southern bridge had not been replaced after the 1920 flood. A solitary girl poses on the path while a number of other children crowd into the rustic shelter. An Empire View Productions, Doncaster card, photograph by Charles Jamson

A Sunday afternoon in Hubbard's Hills about 1910.
Note the newly planted ornamental shrubs in front of the Memorial Fountain.
A Cotswold Publishing Co. hand-coloured photograph.

A similar view in 1936, with the ornamental conifers now shading the pathway in front of the Fountain. Access is by the post-1920 flood replacement footbridge. The eroding river bank on the left has been shored up with timbers

Farm and its land was not part of the purchase.) The trustees also purchased an additional 8 acres 2 roods 34 perches at the south end of the valley, three acres of which being a continuation of Fisher's Hill were fenced and planted with over 8,000 trees – beech, ash, sycamore, larch, Scots pine and spruce to continue the woodland on that side of the valley – by Louth nurseryman George Moody (his nursery was on High Holme Road).

The trustees then set in hand other improvement works, including thinning trees on the east, a controversial move, in order to provide better views of the valley from the top path. That work was carried out by William Havelock, forester to the Earl of Yarborough, and Benjamin Stone, land agent to W H Smythe of Elkington Hall (who also superintended other new work). The reservoir was desilted to a depth of six feet by John Hodgson & Son (of Upgate, Louth) to become an ornamental lake 'to give a clear and strong reflection of the wooded slope', with a wide entrance path and gates on the west side. Trees were also planted there including seven lime trees (one for each of the trustees) which still stand. The top path was levelled and banked, and stiles and other obstructions removed, and steps were made down the steep slope at the south end.

Stepping stones were placed in the river, presented by Sowerby & Co (linseed and cotton seed cake manufacturers) and cascade features created in the river upstream. Three rustic bow bridges were built across the river, one to replace the old footbridge on the main path, and two leading to the Memorial Fountain (a drinking fountain) inside the main bend of the river. The slope behind had to be cut into and shored up with rocks to create a flat area for it. The Memorial is in the form of a portico to a Greek temple, with tesselated pavement, designed by Reginald Fowler (architect son of James Fowler) and built by George Vickers of Queen Street, Louth. The inscription on it records the presentation of Hubbard's Hills 'to the Mayor, Aldermen and Councillors of the Borough of Louth upon certain trusts for the benefit of the people of Louth on the 1st day of August 1907'.

Why did the Pahud trustees choose to use part of the bequest to purchase Hubbard's Hills? There is no record of their discussions, but there are clear clues in the speeches made on the day of the official opening. In handing over the deeds to the Borough Council, the senior trustee and Rector of Louth, Canon Wilde, referred to 'Hubbard's Valley being to us what it had been in the past, such a delightful pleasure garden and such an agreeable park for Louth' and said that it was 'our duty towards that picturesque spot ... to make it a delightful and happy pleasure ground for the good people of Louth'. He also noted that it was 'a very seasonable time for the trustees to come in. Had the idea been carried out which was proposed, the cutting down of the noble trees [beech, ash and a few oak] on the bank side for sale ... the dale and valley would have been certainly ruined'.

In other words, their action was to prevent change, in the form of tree felling by the new owner John Ward, which would have ruined the prospect of the valley as it had been known to at least two generations of Louth people and visitors. In his acceptance speech the Mayor, Councillor Richard Dawson, pledged the Borough Council 'to maintain and uphold it in the same manner as it had been in years past ... in all its pristine beauty for time immemorial'.

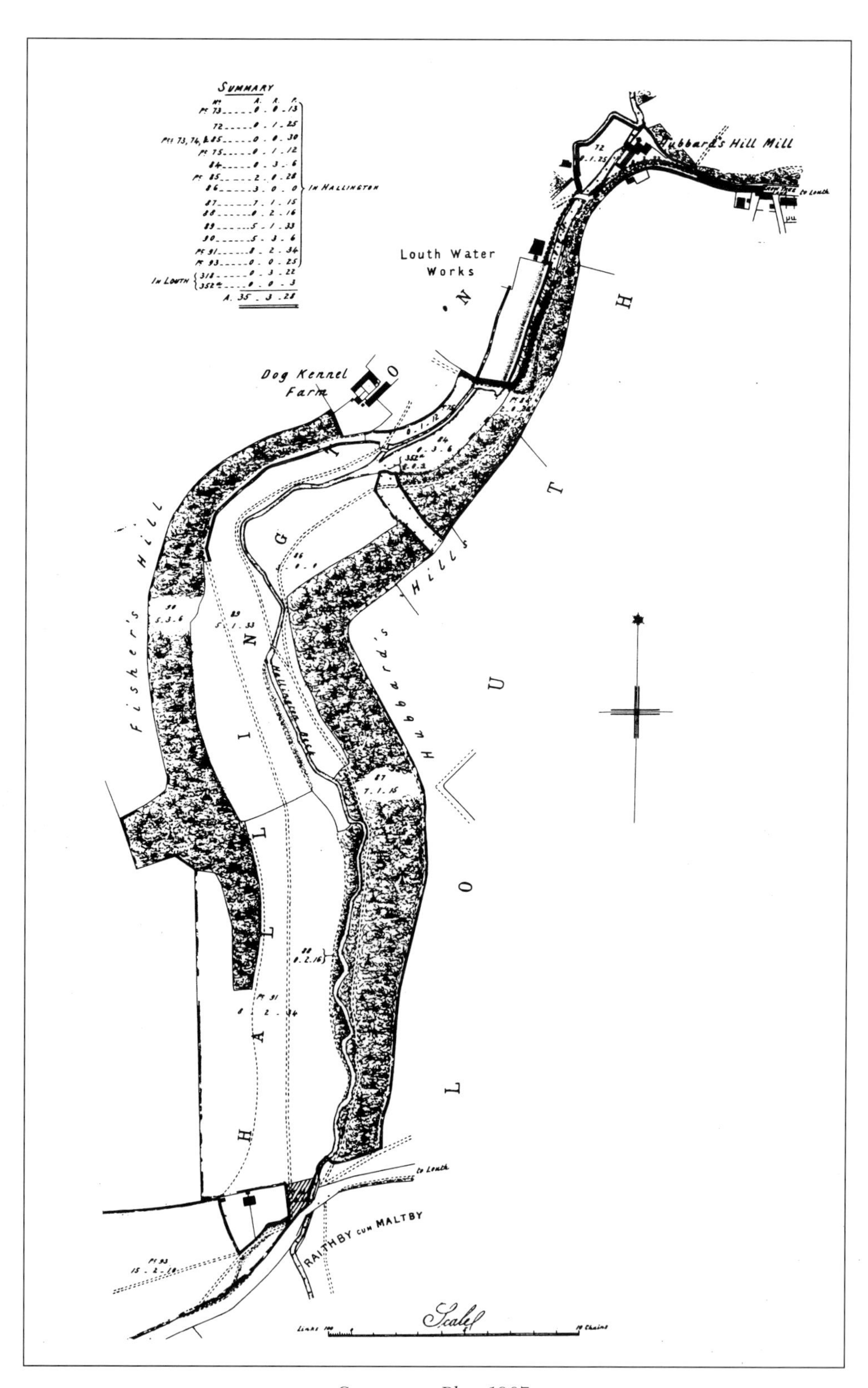

Conveyance Plan 1907

At the Mayor's celebration lunch there was grateful reference made to the money spent by the trustees in putting Hubbard's Hills into 'creditable condition'. Alderman Henry Simpson recalled that he had 'known the hills since boyhood, and did not know there was a single part of the stream that I had not attempted to jump'. Such activity was not specifically banned, but the Schedule to the Conveyance set down a number of conditions for the management of what had become one of the first public country parks in Britain. These are the full seventeen sections of the Schedule.

1. The road leading from Crowtree Lane in Louth through the property as far as the entrance to Dog Kennel Farm is hereafter to be maintained and kept in good order by Louth Town Council.

2. The natural beauty of the property and its rural character is to be forever maintained and no trees are to be felled except when such felling is necessary for the preservation of the remaining trees and all necessary replanting is from time to time to be carried out to, as far as possible, preserve the estate in the same condition as it now is.

3. The Council shall provide a proper supply of drinking water from the Louth Water Company during the summer months for the Memorial Fountain erected by the Pahud Trustees and shall at all times thereafter keep the said fountain in repair.

4. No new footpath is to be made or used through or over the plantation known as Fisher's Hill or any part thereof.

5. As from the 13th May 1908 the portion of the Estate which consists of grassland is to be grazed with sheep only except for any two months between lst October and 13th April in any year, when such land may, in the discretion of the Council as such Trustees be stocked with young store beasts.

6. No grassland is to be ploughed up or meadowed.

7. Subject to any existing tenancy the right of fishing on the property is to be made to one person only at a time for any period not less than one year and not exceeding seven years on condition that such fishing tenant shall only fish for trout with a fly and shall return to the water any fish weighing less than 6 ozs; that each tenant shall not sub-let and that as right to fish shall be sold or given for value by such tenant at any time to any other person or persons.

8. No birds nesting shall be allowed on the Estate and everything shall be done to encourage and preserve wild life on the property.

9. No gun or firearm shall be used or fired on the property.

At the foot of Fisher's Hill, still there today.

Rustic Shelters

*On the east bank towards the south end,
this one was wrecked in the 1920 flood and not replaced.*

10. Dogs shall be kept under proper control and shall not be encouraged or allowed to swim in the reservoir, Mill Dam or stream and no wild life shall in any way be interfered with or disturbed except the killing of foxes, hares or otters in the ordinary course of hunting with hounds, the necessary keeping down of rabbits (which shall be carried out only by digging and using ferrets and nets) and the trapping of moles on the grassland.

11. No bathing shall be allowed in any portion of the stream, reservoir or Mill Dam after 8am on any day and then only under proper regulations to be made by such Louth Town Council as Trustees with the exception that the Council may grant special permission on not more than three days in any one year for any swimming contests to be held under such conditions and within such hours as such Council may determine.

12. No boating shall be allowed on any portion of the stream, reservoir or Mill Dam.

13. The rents and profits derived from the property shall be kept in reserve from time to time as a fund for keeping the property in the same order and repair as it is now in, including the repair of the road and the Memorial Fountain and providing or renewing seats and the provision of roofed shelters with open sides, and the wages of a caretaker, with this exception – that if no caretaker is employed and the property is patrolled by the Borough Police under any arrangement which may be given, the Louth Town Council as Trustees shall have power to pay to the Borough Fund an annual proportion of the rents and profits not exceeding the sum of £20.

14. With the exception of the property known as 'Hubbard's Hill Mill' and premises containing 3 roods 22 perches and any shelters erected under Condition 13, no building shall be erected on the property either permanent or otherwise for any purpose whatever and no shooting galleries, roundabouts, booths, stalls or swings shall at any time be erected, allowed or used on the property and no intoxicating liquor shall ever be sold on the property or any occasional licence applied for for the purpose of the sale thereof thereon.

15. With the exception of horses, no cattle or pigs shall be kept on the said premises known as 'Hubbard's Hill Mill' after the termination of the existing tenancy and nothing shall be permitted or condoned to injuriously affect the stream for fishing purposes, and also manure shall be from time to time removed from such premises.

16. No political, religious or public meeting shall be held or permitted on the property.

17. The Louth Town Council shall make such bye-laws as may be necessary for securing the observation of the foregoing conditions and generally for the regulation of the above property and the preservation of order and prevention of nuisance thereon.

BOROUGH OF LOUTH.

Presentation of

HUBBARD'S HILLS

To the People of Louth.

GREAT REJOICINGS,

Thursday,

August 1st, 1907.

PROGRAMME.

9 to 10 & 11 to 12—CHURCH BELLS RINGING.

12-30.—PUBLIC PRESENTATION in the Town Hall of the TITLE DEEDS to the Estate given to the People of Louth by the late Mr. Pahud's Trustees.

1 to 2.—MILITARY BAND in the Market Place.

2.—CHILDREN WILL MARCH IN PROCESSION to the Hills.

2-30.—CHILDREN'S ENTERTAINMENT, consisting of Living Marionettes, Chinese Conjuring, Ventriloquism, Negro Sketch, Punch and Judy, &c.

3 to 4.—100 yards Swimming Race, 50 yards Plank Swimming, Walking the Greasy Pole. Prizes 15s., 10s., 5s. for each event. Regulation Dress will be provided. Entries to the Hon. Secs. up to the time of the event.

4-30 to 5-30.—TEA FOR CHILDREN, as arranged by the respective School Authorities in Mr. Lamming's Field.

6 to 9.—**VARIETY ENTERTAINMENT,** supplied by WILL TEMPLE, the Universal Amusement Caterer, Nottingham. French & Angelo in their marvellous Aerial Feats over the Stage. Wheelo, the American Tramp Cyclist, smart, clever, funny. Stanfield's Performing Dogs, clever canine wonders. Clown Viddle and his Blondin Donkey. Tell and Tell, Acrobats and Stilt Walkers. Mons. Tello, the Clown Juggler. The Two Butwyns in their Burlesque Musical Act. Temple's Punch, Judy and Toby (3 performances).

2-30 to 5 & 6 to 9.—

The BABBINGTON MILITARY BAND

will play Selections in the Valley.

To conclude with a Magnificent Display of

FIREWORKS!!

By Messrs. Brock & Co., London, the gift of

HIS WORSHIP THE MAYOR

(Councillor R. Dawson).

The Committee have made arrangements with a Contractor to provide

Plain & Meat Teas and other Refreshments,

at reasonable charges.

GOD SAVE THE KING.

GEORGE BLAZE, ROBERT PICKERING, THOS. FALKNER ALLISON, } Joint Hon. Secs.

HERBERT C. BENTLEY, Hon. Treas.

None of these conditions inhibited the Great Rejoicings when Hubbard's Hills was presented to the people of Louth on Thursday Ist August 1907. The church bells were rung from 9am to 10am and from 11 to noon, when all shops closed (Thursday was the normal half-day closing). At 12.30 the title deeds were formally handed over at a ceremony in the Town Hall. Crowds filled the Market Place including nearly 2,000 children, virtually the total school population of the town, marshalled by Malachi Bice, headmaster of the Eastfield Road School, who conducted the children singing. The Babbington Military Band played until two o'clock and then with the Church Lads' Brigade bugle band led the children to Hubbard's Hills. A stage had been set up in the natural amphitheatre in front of Fisher's Hill and the children were entertained by Living Marionettes, Chinese Conjuring, Ventriloquists, a Negro Sketch and Punch and Judy.

From 3 o'clock to 4 o'clock there were swimming races in the reservoir – 100 yards and 50 yards 'plank swimming', and Walking the Greasy Pole, with prizes of 15, 10 and 5 shillings. A tea was provided for the children, in their school groups, in Edward Lamming's field adjoining Dog Kennel Farm. Plain and meat teas and other refreshments were available for adults at 'reasonable charges'. There followed three hours of variety entertainment produced by Will Temple, the Universal Amusement Caterer from Nottingham. Acts included trapeze artists French and Angelo, Wheelo the American tramp cyclist, Stanfield's performing dogs, Clown Viddle and his Blondin Donkey, acrobats and stilt walkers Tell and Tell, Tello the clown juggler and a burlesque musical by The Two Butwyns. The Babbington Military Band was also playing elsewhere in the valley.

As darkness fell the crowd was entertained with the wonderful new cinematograph, and the day concluded with fireworks and set-piece pyrotechnics by Brock & Co ending with the legend in letters of fire MAY LOUTH ENJOY HUBBARDS HILLS. A newspaper reporter estimated that there were some 8,000 people in Hubbard's Hills that day. The town must have been almost empty as the population at that time was about 9,700.

At the speech making earlier in the day the local Member of Parliament, Robert William (later Sir Robert) Perks 'supposed the young people of Louth would continue to wander as in days of old up to Hubbard's Wood for amusement, for exchange of opinions ... and for all sorts of like purposes' (!), and had offered £100 for the construction of two wooden rustic shelters in the valley. Only the one on the west side, opposite the Memorial Fountain, remains. Meanwhile William Bradley Brannick saw the potential of increased numbers visiting the Hills, and drew up plans for tea rooms built of timber at Dog Kennel Farm. They survive, with additions, as today's cafe. He also opened up his own land to groups wishing to camp or hold events not permitted in the valley: the Louth Church Lads' Brigade camped every year in the field behind the farm, and Methodist groups held events there. The tea rooms would have done a good trade on Saturday 22 June 1911, when festivities to celebrate the Coronation of King George V drew large crowds to Hubbard's Hills for stage shows and aquatic sports, recorded by local photographers William Roberts (14 Eastgate) and Henry Burditt (2a Mercer Row).

Schoolchildren sing the Old Hundredth accompanied by the Babbington Military Band on the stage.

1st August 1907
Photographs by W.H. Burditt, Louth

No wonder Louth was nearly empty that afternoon.

Watching the stage entertainment.
Behind the set are the bicycles of Wheelo, the American tramp cyclist.

1st August 1907
Photographs by W.H. Burditt, Louth

On stage are Clown Viddle and his Blondin Donkey.

Walking the Greasy Pole competition

1st August 1907
Photographs by W.E. Roberts, Louth

All in their Sunday best for the children's entertainment

Another Cotswold Publishing Co. hand-coloured view on a Sunday afternoon showing one of the rustic bow bridges for access to the Fountain.

A unusual winter scene in the same location soon after the 1920 flood which swept away the rustic rails of the bow bridge. This was sent as a Christmas card in 1922.

Looking downstream, about 1908.

The Stepping Stones

Looking upstream, with simple wooden rail, mid 1930s.

MANAGEMENT of the park in the early years was low key, patrolled by a caretaker, costs being met by £40-£50 rental income from the watermill and grazing. Doubtless the park was visited by soldiers stationed in and around Louth during the Great War. Then disaster struck on the afternoon of 29 May 1920 – the flash flood which claimed 23 lives in Louth. Over 4$^{1}/_{2}$ inches of rain fell within the 22 square miles catchment area of the River Lud to the west of Louth, depositing some 12 million tons of water in less than three hours. The Tathwell and Hallington Becks combined to turn the stream through the Hubbard's Hills valley into a raging and debris-laden torrent fifteen feet deep. It wrecked the bridge on Halfpenny Lane, washed away the rustic shelter on the east bank and the rustic footbridges, drowned cattle and swept all before it. The torrent also took away the settling tanks of the Waterworks before joining the swollen Welton Beck in Westgate Fields and carving a path of destruction through the town. Mrs Edith Brannick saw and heard the rushing waters from the safety of Dog Kennel Farm. The flood waters also damaged the watermill, which ceased working soon afterwards and became a private house.

In the aftermath of the flood new footbridges had to be built, flat rather than bowed but still with rustic sides, but the east rustic shelter was not replaced. It would also appear that measures were taken to improve the flow of water by removing the riffles and cascades, shoring up the river bend by the Memorial Fountain, and generally containing the river in one course. Also a handrail was installed at the stepping stones. By the 1930s the northern entrance had a more formal look with a clipped laurel hedge by the seven limes, but the view into the valley was still open, while the plantings in front of the Memorial Fountain had grown up and tended to give it a partly enclosed feel. In her botanical diary for August 1935, Miss Daisy Marsden of Westgate noted on one of her regular visits to check on the watermint growing on the stream bank that 'the city fathers who manage it [Hubbard's Hills] like to see things "tidy" ... so the grass is kept cut fairly close and with it goes the mint.' Cutting was by scythe. However, despite the ornamental tendencies, the valley remained very much a rural scene.

Kelly's Lincolnshire Directory entries for Louth in the 1920s and early 1930s recorded Hubbard's Hills as in Hallington parish, 'a natural park finely situated in the form of a gorge between well-wooded hills ... held by the Corporation in trust ... and used as a public park'. However, that part of Hallington was transferred to the Borough of Louth under the Parts of Lindsey Review Order 1936. About the same time the Corporation purchased Westgate Fields (12 acres) at the winding up of the estate of Frederick William Bennett of Elmhirst, Crowtree Lane (who died in 1933) 'for public walks and pleasure grounds'. This was in fact a confirmation of what had virtually been the practice for many years.

Botanist Daisy Marsden was also a regular visitor to Westgate Fields. In July 1937 she noted in her diary: 'A few months ago some of us were very much amazed when the Corporation decided to fill up a gulley [created by the 1920 flood] in the Westgate Fields by using it as a "rubbish tip". It was very unsightly for some weeks, but now it is levelled and quickly becoming covered with vegetation and bids fair to become a happy hunting ground for botanists. This evening [12th] I saw – besides the usual weeds, willowherb etc – one blue linum, 5-6 opium

continued on page 62

Singing the National Anthem
Is the photographer on the stage (who hasn't taken his cap off) Henry Burditt?

Coronation Festivities 22 June 1911
Photographs by W.E. Roberts, Louth

Children's entertainment: a pierrot, and the box behind is for Punch and Judy.
Note planks for the children to sit on.

Coronation Festivities 22 June 1911

Jack Clement's Concert Party from Mablethorpe

Photographs by W.E. Roberts, Louth

Coronation Festivities 22 June 1911

The setting of the stage in front of Fisher's Hill between the main bridge and the Memorial Fountain.

Photographs by Henry Burditt, Louth

The road over the reservoir dam to Dog Kennel Farm about 1903. It shows how much the reservoir had silted up with vegetation growing on the silt and only a winding channel of water. Published in a book of Picturesque Louth by William Fieldhouse, stationer, 13 Mercer Row. A postcard version carried this message on the back: 'How would this suit to have a spoon round here at night'.

The road to the farm about 1910 shows the brick bridge repaired with new fencing and iron railings on the other side, and the reservoir dredged with new entrance path alongside.

1904

The Reservoir becomes The Lake

1908

1918

The Lake

1960s

Feeding the swans, 1936. Mrs Hilda Horton with (L-R)
Bill Barker, Betty Horton, Dick Barker, Gwen Barker and Bob Horton.
Photograph by Mrs Dorothy Barker

Only two swans on the reservoir in 1912.

Dog Kennel Farm
early 1920s

Farm and Tearooms (right) seen from the Devil's Walk

Church Lads' Brigade

A Methodist group

Wildlife Watch on Fisher's Hill, September 1999

poppies, several potato and fair quantity of canary grass'. Then on 27 July: '41 flowering plants recorded – most extraordinary collection of weeds and garden throw-outs'. Visiting again in August 1938, her diary note reads: 'In first Westgate field World's-end Close, where they filled in hollow last year, has appeared a large crop of inkcap mushrooms, both shaggy-cap and common ink-cap ... those near the path are quickly destroyed by passers by, but those up the old gulley fare better ... much "ink" is spilt already'.

At Hubbard's Hills in the 1930s, Fred Whitworth of Dog Kennel Farm was running the refreshment rooms. The Silver Jubilee of King George V and Queen Mary in 1935 was marked by a new plantation in the central section of the valley, on the west side of the river near a line of old horsechestnut trees.

Otter hunting was still active in the area in the 1930s. John Wightman of Maltby House was master, huntsman and secretary of the East Lincolnshire Otterhounds with kennels at Maltby Wood. It was a pack of twelve hounds, half foxhound and half pure-bred otterhounds. Hunting was on Mondays and Thursdays and occasional Tuesdays, around Louth and Market Rasen, but it is not known whether the pack entered Hubbard's Hills – which was allowed under section ten of the Schedule to the Conveyance.

Management work in the 1960s included the necessary periodic dredging of the lake in 1962, and extensive tree thinning in 1964 to encourage new growth and age diversity. The 1968 edition of the Ordnance Survey recorded a landscape which was becoming wilder and less ornamental. General access had been improved with more bridges over the river, and there were public conveniences at the north entrance, although car parking there was still on private property. There was a small public parking area at the south entrance.

When the Lincolnshire Wolds were designated as an Area of Outstanding Natural Beauty (AONB) in April 1973, the boundary to the west of Louth was carefully drawn to include Hubbard's Hills, which received special mention in the 1993 Landscape Assessment by the Countryside Commission. Two years earlier Hubbard's Hills had been designated a Regionally Important Geomorphological Site by the Lincolnshire Wildlife Trust. A key aim of the Management Plan for the AONB, drawn up by the Lincolnshire Wolds Countryside Service, is to sustain and maintain the natural beauty and landscape character of the Wolds as a whole including significant features such as Hubbard's Hills.

When the long debated and awaited A16 bypass for Louth came to fruition in 1990-91, it was routed to the west of Hubbard's Hills. It is in a cutting through the chalk, curving east across the south end of the valley on a bridge over Halfpenny Lane and the Hallington Beck. In order to help baffle traffic noise the Bypass Plantation was established on the former open grass slope at the southern end of the valley.

At local government reorganisation in 1974, management of Hubbard's Hills and Westgate Fields had passed to East Lindsey District Council under a Joint Committee with Louth Town Council. Several mature trees were lost in the severe gale of October 1988, and there was a selective felling scheme in 1998.

Louth Town Council retained responsibility for Hubbard's Hill Mill which had ceased working in the 1920s and been converted to a private house, and the former mill race had been dammed up and made into an attractive garden. It became vacant and the Council was looking for a new tenant or a new use. In 1995 the Lincolnshire Wildlife Trust undertook a study of the property with a view to developing it as a field studies and interpretation centre for Hubbard's Hills, but this proved not to be feasible. Eventually the Town Council disposed of it, and a link was broken with the original purchase by the Pahud trustees. However, in 1998, the Golden Jubilee year of the Widlife Trust, the Louth Area Group of the Trust published *The Lenten Ottaway Walk: a nature ramble round Hubbard's Hills* which identified the main flora and fauna to be found there. Lenten Ottaway was a founder member of the Trust, a true field naturalist who had known the Hills well and who had died in 1995 at the age of 82.

Another link between Westgate Fields and Hubbard's Hills was created with the launch of the Louth Art Trail in 2002, a Louth Town Council initiative with support from the District and County Councils and East Midlands Arts and Lottery and European funding. In addition to contemporary sculptures in the town, in Westgate Fields artist Howard Bowcott was inspired by the natural setting to create an arboretum of sculptures: four giant wooden tree leaves which function as lookouts, seats and picnic tables on the upper slopes.

Two years earlier at the Millennium another feature had been installed in Westgate Fields alongside the traditional path to Hubbard's Hills: a Sundial of Human Involvement. This was provided by the Rotary Club of Louth as a reminder that Louth is one of the few towns in the world on the Greenwich Meridian from which world time is measured. Standing on the central slab set in the turf the time could be told by where one's shadow pointed in the semicircle of number slabs, the position of which indicated both Greenwich Mean and British Summer Time.

By the late 1990s Hubbard's Hills park was showing signs of suffering from increasing visitor pressure and lack of adequate management. In 1999 a Regeneration Group was formed with membership from Town and District Councils and representatives of interested local organisations to discuss how it might be possible to restore the park to a more natural and biodiverse state which for so long had been its attraction. A conservation and management plan was commissioned with the aim of reversing the decline in the quality of the landscape and to bid for funding from the Heritage Lottery Fund's Urban Parks Programme. The plan prepared by consultants Sheils Flynn identified three main zones: the entrance area at the north end, the central recreation zone and the more natural area at the southern end. For each zone the threats were seen as declining ecological diversity, erosion of landscape quality, recreational overload, inadequate access and poor drainage.

After two phases of public consultation, the following proposals were made. Entrance zone: open up views into the valley, redesign the river weir, refurbish the toilet block and incorporate an interpretation facility, improve the access path, reprofile the lake to encourage emergent wetland vegetation, and provide a bridge to the east bank. Recreation zone: enhance riverbank habitats, re-create

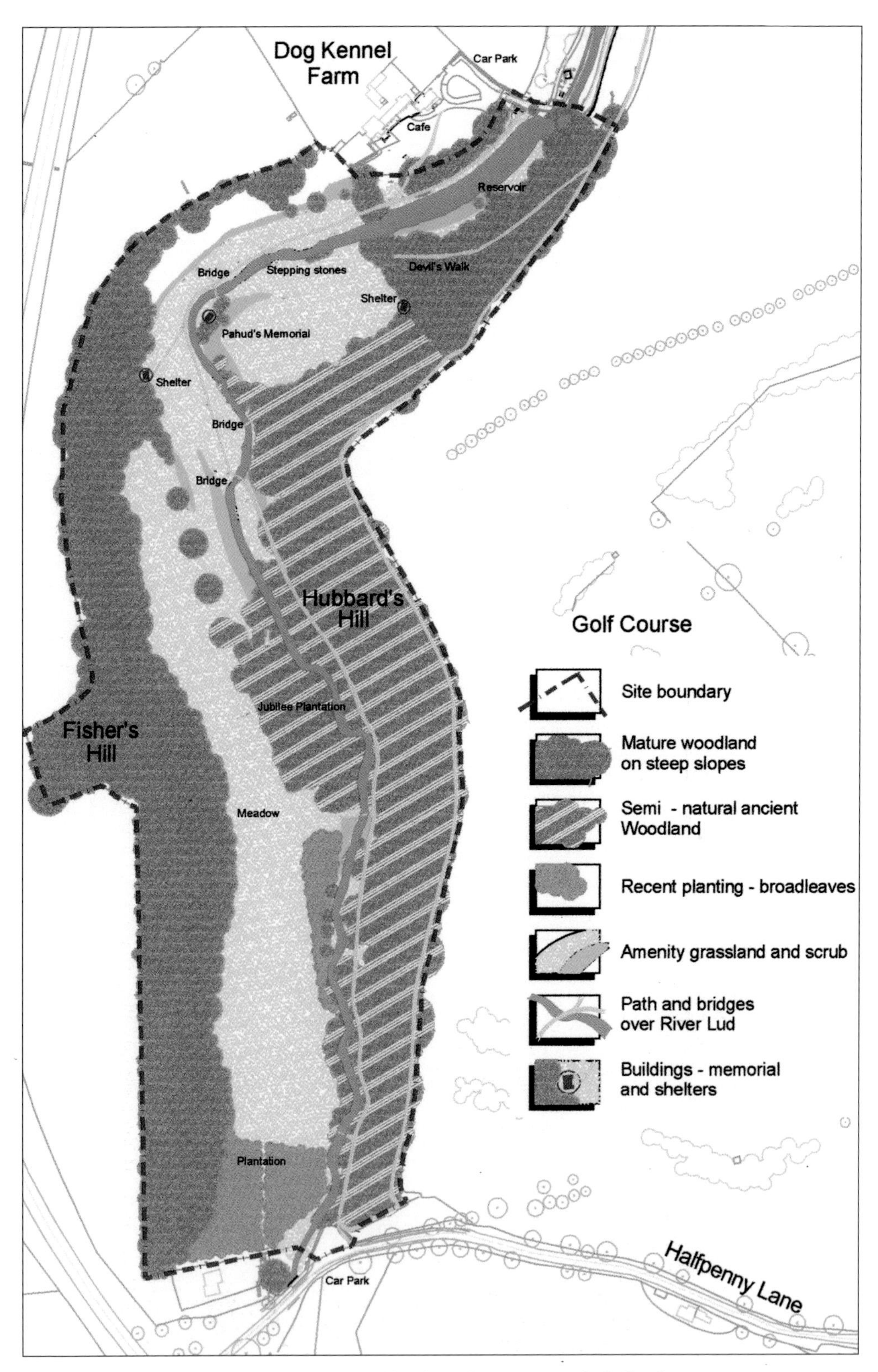

Principal features of Hubbard's Hills (Courtesy of Sheils Flynn)

a wildflower meadow on the east slope, re-establish a drainage ditch on the west side, enhance footpath connections to viewpoints, repair the Pahud Memorial Fountain and improve access to it and landscape surrounding it. Natural area: re-introduce lost river and riverside habitats, and restore the floristic wildlife of the meadow grassland. In addition to employ a warden or ranger to provide an interpretation and education service, and to combat vandalism and enhance security for users of the park.

The full report and proposals with maps and artist's impressions was ready in June 2005, carrying an overall price tag of £2.45 million. There were however health and safety and disability access issues to be resolved before further progress could be made. There were by then serious concerns that the proposals went too far and would result in Hubbard's Hills losing its rural character and sense of naturalness. Although it was clear that some urgent management action was necessary, the view was that it should be more limited, and a small group of local people, The Friends of Hubbard's Hills, produced their own analysis and suggestions for action before the 2007 centenary. Improvements to the river are a long term responsibility of the Environment Agency under the Lincolnshire Chalk Streams Project, and some initial work at Hubbard's Hills had already been started.

The District Council prepared its own concepts for a limited first stage regeneration scheme, funded by the Council. These related to the north access path, treatment of the west riverbank upstream from the stepping stones, repair of the Memorial Fountain, repair and refurbishment of bridges, treatment of paths and fencing on the Devil's Walk, provision of more seating, and signage at the south entrance. These were the subject of public consultations and amendment in autumn 2006. Works were put in hand and should be completed for the centenary on lst August 2007.

Cover illustration on W. Mawer's booklet, 1884

The only known photograph of the Hallington Beck meandering through the field on the south side of Halfpenny Lane before tumbling into the Valley between the woods of Fisher's Hill (left) and Hubbard's Hill. The rising ground to the right of the Beck marks the limit of ice advance which caused the permanent diversion of the stream through the Valley. Published about 1895 in 'Sleights Photographic View Album of Louth' and sold by James Sleight in his fancy repository, Market Place, Louth.

The view in 2001 of Hubbard's Hills and the A16 bypass from the top of Stanmore Hill on the road to Horncastle.

The Lenten Ottaway Walk

A nature ramble round Hubbard's Hills

1 Walk down the slope to the river, the **Hallington Beck,** a major tributary of the River Lud, here dammed to form a small lake. It is a chalk stream and therefore never freezes. Here are **moorhen** and **mallard,** with a few farm ducks. In winter there are often **black-headed gulls** although at that time of year not with black heads but just a black spot behind the eye.

Mallard

2 Go through the gate by **sycamore** and **ash** trees and walk along the river to the bridge. On the slope to the right the chalk can be seen between the stumps of trees which had to be felled. This area has recently been replanted.

Ash

3 Cross the footbridge to the **Fountain Temple,** often called 'The Folly'. Here is a plaque which tells how the 36 acre estate came to be given to the town. Auguste Alphonse Pahud came to Louth from Switzerland and for a short time taught at King Edward V1 Boys' Grammar School before marrying Annie Grant of Withern. Twelve years later she died suddenly and Pahud was so heartbroken that he took his own life. Part of the trust fund he left was used to purchase Hubbard's Hills for the town in memory of his wife. Restoration of the temple is part of the management plan for the Hills.

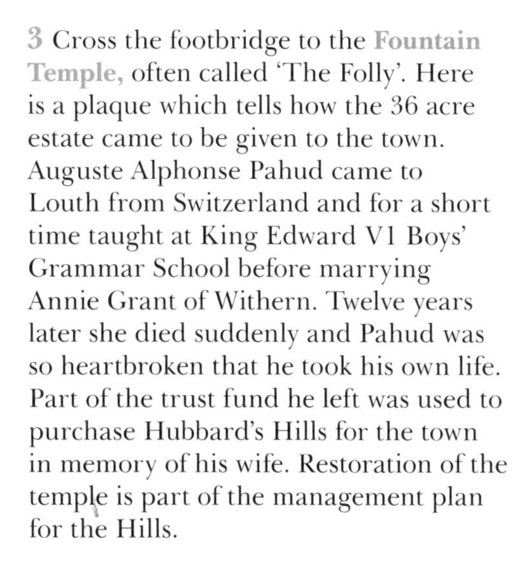

Sycamore

4 Recross the bridge and walk round the bend in the river, fast flowing at this point. **Kingfishers** and **dippers** can be seen here, and **meadowsweet** and **soft rush** grow with **water forget-me-not** and **water figwort.** In spring look for **hazel** catkins – 'lambs tails' – shedding their pollen. **Water voles** (Kenneth Grahame's 'Ratty') can sometimes be seen. Leave the main path and walk over to the wooden shelter. With so much tree cover this is a good place to look for birds. By the stream are **willows, sycamore, sloe** and a dense undergrowth of **bramble.** Above and behind are fine stands of **beech** with an understorey of **elderberry** and **sycamore.** Here are many common birds such as **wren, chaffinch, blue tit** and **great tit, robin** and **blackbird** to be seen and heard, as well as seasonal visitors such as **brambling** in the autumn feeding on beechmast.

Water Vole

Blue tit

5 Now walk along the wood edge where at different times of year you can see **wood avens, cuckoo pint, ground ivy** and the dainty grass, **wood melick.** There has been infill planting of **beech** and some **oak.** In and on the edge of the wood are dead and decaying tree trunks. If you press them in some places they will be soft and spongy where insects are living and feeding. On the outside are **bracket** and other **fungi,** sometimes the attractive **fairies' bonnets.** The skirt of the woodland has been left unmown to encourage wild flowers and insects as food for birds and butterflies. Note the **elderberry** – food for birds, and the **nettles** – food for **tortoiseshell** and **peacock** butterflies.

Beech

Peacock

Small tortoiseshell

6 In the centre of the large mown area is a line of **horsechestnut** trees. Walk back to these and join the path which goes through the Jubilee Plantation above the river. This was planted in 1935 to celebrate the Silver Jubilee of King George V and Queen Mary. **Tawny owls** nest here, but not in any numbers as owls are very territorial and do not tolerate intruders. A **great spotted woodpecker** pays the occasional visit here. In the summer a large area of the aptly named **enchanter's nightshade** can be seen.

Horsechestnut

Great spotted woodpecker

7 Beyond the Jubilee Plantation is a new area of mixed trees and bushes including **cherry, hazel, wild rose, poplar, beech** and **oak.** While the trees are young notice the amount of ground cover plants compared with the bare ground under mature trees. The valley is now opening out. Molehills are to be seen – heaps of fine soil with all the worms removed by scavenging **moles.** This wide grassy area is a favourite grazing ground for **rabbits,** particularly in the early morning and evening. Walk along the riverbank to the footbridge; here willows line the bank – **weeping willow** with its drooping branches and the more upright **crack willow.** Beyond the open grassy area is the Bypass Plantation, an attempt to muffle the noise from the bypass which curves round to the west of the Hills.

Wild rose

Mole

8 Cross the footbridge where there is an information board about the trees and bushes and a description of the formation of the valley. The flow of the river is slower here because of the bends and water plants have a chance to grow on the banks – **watercress, water figwort** and **water forget-me-not.**

Oak

9 Now climb the steps up the side of the valley. On either side are bushes of **sloe** and **hawthorn** festooned with **ivy.** The presence of **dog's mercury** among the trees indicates an ancient woodland. Turn left at the sign and walk along the top path by the edge of the beech hanger, noticing the shallow roots of the trees so easily damaged by trampling. In autumn **grey squirrels** and flocks of **pigeons** can be seen enjoying the beech nuts. To the right is the golf course with its formal planting. As the path swings to the right and loses height **larch, ash, elderberry** and ivy-clad **hawthorn** fill a gap in the beeches. **Ivy** has its flowers in autumn, and berries in winter to provide food for birds.

Dog's mercury

Squirrel

Pied Wagtail

10 The path eventually comes out onto Crowtree Lane. Opposite is the recently restored old watermill house, first built between 1805 and 1823. On the other side of the river is an **osier** bed once used for basketmaking. Between Crowtree Lane and the river is the splendid open space of Westgate Fields. Down by the river are the huge leaves of **butterburr,** and you may see **pied wagtails,** perhaps **herons** looking for fish at the trout farm, and across the river **fallow deer** in the grounds of Thorpe Hall. To return to your start point walk back past the millhouse, cross the bridge over the river where it was diverted by the mill headrace dam, and continue on the path past the 19th century waterworks building designed by the Louth architect James Fowler.

Heron

The Hubbard's Hills Watermill in 1907.

The old mill was converted into a private house and the mill race drained and made into an attactive garden in the 1930s. The exposed waterwheel is on the left of the building.

HUBBARD'S HILLS

From " Thoughts in Verse," by Two Friends
Louth (1896)

By C. DONNER
(*Known as* " The Postman Poet")

THAN " Hubbard's Hills " a fairer spot
Can scarce be found in Lincoln's shire :
Majestic are their tree-crowned heights,
Fit scene to rouse a poet's fire.
How lovely are their mossy slopes
When sweetly scented wildflower bloom,
Breathing upon the balmy air
Their wondrous wealth of rich perfume !
How fairy-like their winding dell,
The Lud's clear waters murmuring through ;
Where in the spring-time gaily grow
Forget-me-nots of lovely hue.
O verdant hills ! surpassing fair,
Your pleasant groves I love to tread,
And listen to your full-voiced choir,
A grassy carpet 'neath me spread.
And who that wants a cool retreat
From noontide's scorching heat,
Would not delight to seek your shade,
And sit where leafy branches meet.
O, sweet seclusion ! where the soul
May find a respite from earth's toil ;
And thus refreshed, may better brave
This life's unceasing, stern turmoil.
Fair hills ! may ye time's change survive,
(Your wondrous beauty unimpaired ;)
Until ye tremble at His voice,
By whom your lofty heights were reared.

THE LATE SPRING IN HUBBARD'S HILLS

THE hazel catkins are smoky yellow,
Palm willows are silver-set,
But here on the hill, only last year's larch cones,
No tassels of scarlet yet.

The elm tree reddens—the beech is lifting
Her slim gold spires to the light,
But down by the reeds, only steel-blue water,
No kingfisher flashing in sight.

What if the clean salt wind be bitter ?
Frost-broken fields lie bare ?
Are not the catkins silver and yellow ?
Are not the elm flowers there ?

E. M. INGOLDBY.

Poetry Club, King Edward VI Girls' Grammar School, 1930